UNITED STATES
Territories

by
LINDA THOMPSON

Rourke
Publishing LLC
Vero Beach, Florida 32964

www.rourkepublishing.com

PHOTO CREDITS:
Courtesy Library of Congress, Prints and Photographs Division: pages 7, 8, 9, 10, 11, 12, 13, 14, 16, 18, 19, 20, 23, 24, 25, 26, 27, 28, 29, 30, 32, 34, 40, 42; Courtesy National Archives and Records Administration: pages 18, 36; Courtesy National Oceanic and Atmospheric Administration: pages 4, 6, 15, 17, 22, 35, 38, 39; Courtesy National Parks Service: Title Page, page 33; Courtesy Rohm Padilla: pages 5, 37; Courtesy U.S. Fish and Wildlife Service: page 11.

SPECIAL NOTE: Further information about people's names shown in the text in bold can be found on page 47. More information about glossary terms in bold can be found on pages 46 and 47.

DESIGN: ROHM PADILLA
LAYOUT/PRODUCTION: LUCY PADILLA

Library of Congress Cataloging-in-Publication Data

Library of Congress Cataloging-in-Publication Data

Thompson, Linda, 1941-
    United States Territories / Linda Thompson.
        p. cm. -- (The expansion of America II)
    Includes bibliographical references (p.   ) and index.
    ISBN 1-59515-515-5 (hardcover : alk. paper)

TITLE PAGE IMAGE
Virgin Islands National Park, U.S. Virgin Islands

Printed in the U.S.A.

TABLE OF CONTENTS

Chapter 1: BEYOND THE 48 STATES

As the United States grew westward after the American Revolution, it added new states following a given pattern. Each new section of frontier land became a U.S. **territory**. When 5,000 free men lived there, they could form a local government. As many as five states could be created out of a territory, but 60,000 residents were required to qualify for statehood. Citizens of every new state had the same rights and freedoms as all U.S. citizens, including the right to a jury trial and to a public education. This pattern was set by the **Northwest Ordinance**, which Congress passed in 1787.

Since the end of the nineteenth century, however, the country has acquired various territories that have not become states. The United States now has more territories than any other country and governs the lives of more than 4.6 million people in these territories.

Jobos Beach near Isabela, Puerto Rico

4

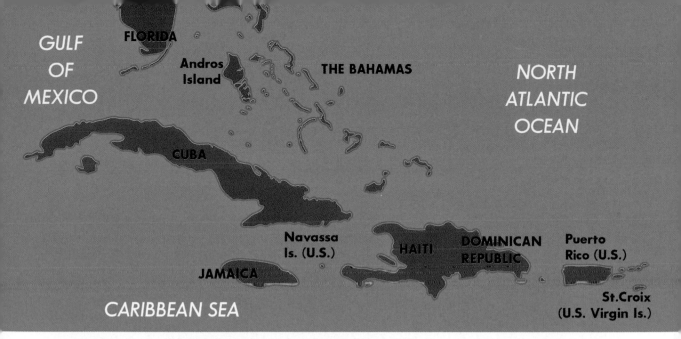

Map of the Caribbean Sea and some U.S. Territories. For territories in the Pacific Ocean, see page 37.

All of these entities are islands in the Caribbean Sea or the Pacific Ocean. They include **Puerto Rico**, the Virgin Islands, **Guam**, the Northern Mariana Islands, and **American Samoa**. The United States also has "**compacts** of free association" with the Federated States of **Micronesia**, the Republic of the Marshall Islands, and the Republic of **Palau**. In addition, a number of tiny islands or groups of islands without permanent populations are called "U.S. possessions."

Some former U.S. possessions are now independent countries. For example, Cuba and the Philippine Islands, "prizes" from the **Spanish American War**, became independent years ago. Two other former territories— Alaska and Hawaii—ended a long statehood struggle by becoming the 49th and 50th states in 1959.

Passing through the Panama Canal

The Spanish-American War made the United States a colonial power for the first time. The war also served to unite the country and repair the enormous damage to national esteem resulting from the **Civil War**. In the Spanish-American War, President **William McKinley** was careful to give high-level commissions to former **Confederate** officers. Officers and enlisted men from the South eagerly volunteered to show their patriotism and courage. Although some Americans spoke out against what they viewed as an undemocratic tendency to expand into faraway places, a general surge in **nationalism** occurred throughout the country. The construction of the Panama Canal (completed in 1914) also enhanced U.S. status abroad and national pride.

Although the people in some territories are U.S. citizens, they cannot vote for the U.S. president and are limited in other respects. In general, territorial subjects live thousands of miles from American shores and are far poorer than citizens of any state. Many of them rely upon U.S. military spending and tourism to keep their economies healthy.

Alaska seemed to be a useless "ice box" to most Americans in the nineteenth century. It was home to about 40,000 Native Americans, including the **Aleut** in the **Aleutian Islands**, the **Inuit** (or **Eskimo**) in the far north, and the **Tlingit** in the southeast section. About a quarter of the state lies north of the **Arctic Circle**, where much of the soil is permanently frozen and daylight is not visible for

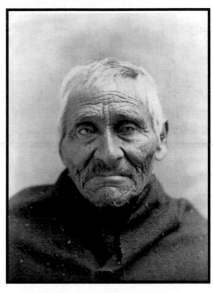

A Tlingit man in Alaska

months at a time. Temperatures in the northern parts of Alaska can average 10 degrees F (-12 degrees C) in the summer and colder than -60 degrees F (-51 degrees C) in the winter!

Eskimo children in fur clothing

William H. Seward

Russia had claimed Alaska since 1741, when fur traders from that country discovered that sea otter and fur seal pelts from Alaskan waters could be sold for high profits. In 1867 Russia surprised the United States by offering Alaska for sale. **William H. Seward**, secretary of state under President **Andrew Johnson**, drew up an agreement for the purchase.

Congress was not enthusiastic. Only a few hundred Americans—mostly miners—had ever visited Alaska. People thought Seward was foolish to even consider it, and the proposal became known as "Seward's **Folly**." Nevertheless, the Senate voted in favor of the purchase, and on July 14, 1868, the House of Representatives **appropriated** $7.2 million to buy Alaska.

President Andrew Johnson

Because of its scant population, Alaska was managed by the army as a "customs and military district" rather than made a territory. American fur trading and salmon canning companies began to do some business there. They did not bring settlers because native workers or seasonal employees could be hired. The Alaska Commercial Company (ACC) was given a 20-year **monopoly** on the seal trade. The Alaska Packers Association in San Francisco controlled 90 percent of the cannery business by 1895. Therefore, economic development took place in Alaska without increases in population. By 1880, of the 33,426 people in Alaska, only 430 were non-native.

An Eskimo fur trader

Poster for a play, *Heart of the Klondike*

Gold discoveries in southeastern Alaska brought a few hundred settlers, including missionaries. Another gold strike in 1896 brought 40,000 American miners to the Klondike region of Alaska and Canada. This strike caused a border dispute between the United States and Great Britain, which was resolved in favor of the United States in 1903.

JACK LONDON

In 1897, an American writer, **Jack London**, headed to Alaska to make his fortune. Instead of gold, he "mined" his adventures there to produce novels and short stories that became widely read. His books such as *The Call of the Wild* (1903) and *White Fang* (1906) fascinated readers and taught them about "the frozen North."

In 1898-99, more gold was found in Nome on the Seward Peninsula, and the non-native population quickly grew to 12,488. By 1900 the population of Alaska was 63,592, of which 48 percent were non-native. In 1898

A man pans for gold on Nome Beach.

Congress extended the **Homestead Act** of 1862 to Alaska. This Act gave 160 acres (65 hectares) of land to settlers who would live on it and improve it for at least five years. In 1906 the "district" was named a "territory." Alaska was now allowed to send a delegate—who could not vote—to Congress.

The army built forts along the Yukon River and a telegraph system. A settlement in the north, Fairbanks, became the largest town by 1905. Investors poured money into railroads, mines, and steamship companies. In 1912, Congress permitted Alaskan voters to elect a state legislature, although it could not regulate resources or change the tax system. Most businesses were still owned by outsiders, who did not want the taxes and regulation of industry that statehood would bring.

The Yukon Delta National Wildlife Refuge, Alaska

In the early twentieth century, the Alaska Railroad was built, Anchorage was founded, and copper mining began. Mt. McKinley National Park was designated in 1917. Big game hunting (caribou, moose, bears, and mountain sheep) became popular. Canned salmon became an important food export to Europe during World War I (1914-1918). Alaskans provided 6.6 million cases of salmon in 1918, yielding $51 million. Coal mining also became a key industry.

After World War I, however, these markets largely vanished, and **inflation** made Alaska an expensive place for doing business. The territory's population fell from 64,356 in 1910 to 55,036 in 1920. As the petroleum industry developed, industry and the military switched from coal to oil. Alaska's economy headed downward, only to be saved by military spending as World War II approached.

A salmon cannery in Alaska

Dutch Harbor Naval Operating Base and Fort Mears, Unalaska Bay, Alaska.

As Japanese aggression became a worldwide threat in the 1930s, political and military leaders urged Congress to build more bases in Alaska, which was close to both Russia and Japan. In 1940 and 1941, $48 million was designated for airfields alone. Military families moved in, and the population ballooned to 233,000 by 1943! The center of population shifted from southeastern Alaska, where fishing and gold mining had prevailed, to the railroad corridor between Anchorage and Fairbanks. Many newcomers remained in Alaska and helped build it toward statehood.

An A-20 attack bomber on an airstrip at Nome, Alaska

Like Alaska, Hawaii could only be reached by sea in the nineteenth century. But unlike Alaska, Hawaii had an organized population and a thriving economy. American businessmen had followed missionaries there after 1820 and started a profitable sugar industry. By the 1840s five of every six ships that stopped at the islands were from the United States. In 1893 the American companies backed a revolution that overthrew Hawaii's queen. They asked the U.S. government to **annex** Hawaii, and it became a U.S. territory in 1898.

Harvesting sugarcane, Hawaii

With territorial status, sugar production grew from 150,000 tons (136,000 metric tons) a year in 1895 to 426,000 tons (386,300 metric tons) in 1904. **James D. Dole** went to Hawaii in 1899 and two years later created the Hawaiian Pineapple Company. One of his employees, **Henry Ginaca**, designed a machine that

A pineapple plant with ripening fruit

could peel, core, and slice 100 pineapples a minute! By 1912, Dole was producing a million cases a year of canned pineapple.

U.S. **legislators** hesitated to make Hawaii a state in the early years. Most Americans opposed Asian immigration. In 1890 Hawaii's population included about 22 percent Chinese and 20 percent Japanese people. They were workers who had been brought in by sugarcane growers. In the early 1900s, with the acquisition of the Philippines after the Spanish-American War, U.S. companies also began bringing large numbers of Filipinos to plant and harvest sugarcane.

A Japanese-American family in Hawaii

In 1900 Congress created a territorial government with an elected legislature, a **judiciary** branch, and a governor, appointed by the U.S. president. Hawaii could send a nonvoting delegate to the House of Representatives. Within 40 years, Hawaii's population grew from 154,000 to 428,000. Hawaii's citizens voted in favor of statehood several times, but Congress rejected their bid. Anti-Asian feelings were very strong, and many people refused to buy Hawaiian sugar because of **prejudice**.

Asians born in Hawaii were citizens of the United States, however, and could vote upon reaching age 21. During the 1920s and 30s, more and more Asian Americans reached voting age and ran for territorial office. The sugar and pineapple industries had strengthened Hawaii's economy, and growers paid significant federal taxes. Between 1900 and 1937, Hawaii sent $144 million more to the United States than it received in benefits.

Five American companies controlled the sugar and pineapple industries, as well as the shipping lines. Known as "the Big Five," they included Castle & Cooke (Dole), Alexander & Baldwin, American Factors, the Theodore H. Davies Co., and C. Brewer & Co. The Big Five became strong **advocates** of statehood, which would allow Hawaii to represent their interests in Congress. In 1935 the House of Representatives scheduled the first hearings on statehood.

Like Alaska, Hawaii was seen as very important to U.S. defense. By 1940 it had become one of the most heavily fortified U.S. military sites. The navy moved its **Pacific Fleet** headquarters to **Pearl Harbor** on the island of **Oahu**, building forts to protect the ships, and bringing about 43,000 U.S. troops to the islands by 1940.

An aerial view of Pearl Harbor

Roosevelt signing the declaration of war against Japan

On December 7, 1941, Japanese bombers attacked the U.S. fleet in Pearl Harbor. That day President **Franklin Roosevelt** asked Congress to declare war against Japan. Congress did not hesitate. Hawaii's legislature tried to prevent Congress from taking control of Hawaii, but instead **martial law** was imposed. Congress and American voters feared that the 158,000 Japanese Americans in Hawaii might have assisted the enemy.

Bombing of the USS *Shaw* in Pearl Harbor, December 7, 1941

Martial law remained in effect until October 1944, even though a commission found that no Hawaiians or Japanese-Hawaiians were involved in bombing Pearl Harbor. Everyone in Hawaii was fingerprinted and placed under military supervision. The government read mail and monitored phone calls. A general curfew and blackout were in force every night. Businesses and stores refused to serve Japanese-Hawaiians, and many lost their jobs.

Although about 1,000 Japanese were taken to **internment** camps on the mainland, most of Hawaii's Japanese and Japanese-Americans were not removed. Political, business, and military leaders worked to minimize the impact on Hawaii's population. Although they had to give up belongings such as short wave radios and firearms, they were not treated as badly as Japanese on the mainland during World War II.

Relocation efforts in San Francisco

THE 442nd REGIMENT

Most Japanese Americans in Hawaii could not serve in the military, but one group became a famous fighting unit—the 100th Infantry Battalion. One member, **Sakae Takahashi**, said, "We're fighting two wars. One for American democracy, and one against the prejudice toward us in America." In 1943, another Japanese American unit was formed, the 442nd Regimental Combat Team.

These units fought in Europe, winning more decorations than any other unit of the same size during the war. By January 1944, service restrictions on Japanese Americans were removed.

Members of the 442nd Regimental Combat Team salute the flag.

By June 1944, Hawaii's population had grown to 859,000. More than 47 percent of these people worked in the military. Civilian construction workers also flowed in to build roads, buildings, airfields, and radio towers. With martial law, however, local wages had been frozen. Seeing that newcomers were taking the better jobs, Hawaiians resolved to change the situation. Although by 1946, 60 percent of Americans favored statehood, it took another 13 years of hard work. Hawaii's eventual success would be tied to statehood efforts in Alaska, 2,500 miles (4,023 km) to the north.

In 1946, it seemed that both Alaska and Hawaii might win statehood because of their contributions to American defense. But instead, the **Cold War** interfered. In Hawaii, workers had formed unions. Some union leaders were sympathetic to the **Communist Party**, further strengthening mainland suspicions about Asian-American loyalty.

Alaska helped Hawaii overcome these obstacles by itself taking aggressive steps toward statehood. The United States could not logically admit one without the other. In 1955-56 Alaska produced and **ratified** a state constitution. Finally, in 1958-59, Congress made Alaska the 49th state and Hawaii the 50th. President **Dwight Eisenhower** signed both bills, which were then endorsed by each territory's voters. Alaskans approved statehood by 5 to 1 and Hawaiians by 17 to 1.

Chapter III: THE SPANISH–AMERICAN WAR AND THE CARIBBEAN

Spain had lost its vast American empire during the first half of the nineteenth century. By 1898, only Cuba and Puerto Rico remained. But Spain also still owned the Philippines, Guam, and other colonies such as the Caroline and Marshall Islands in the Pacific Ocean.

Cuba is just over 100 miles (160 km) south-southeast of Florida, and Puerto Rico lies about 1,000 miles (1,600 km) southeast of Florida. The United States had become Cuba's largest sugar market, purchasing nearly 70 percent of its annual crop. American corporations were heavily invested in plantations, mines, railroads, and other businesses. Because these businessmen wanted to protect their interests, the United States had tried more than once to buy Cuba from Spain. In 1848 President **James K. Polk** offered $100 million for the island, but Spain refused.

The rolling countryside near Santa Clara, Cuba

Puerto Rico was another important producer of sugarcane, coffee, and tobacco. Growing tired of Spanish repression and taxes, both Puerto Ricans and Cubans rebelled in 1868. Spanish

Coffee drying in Puerto Rico

troops quickly put down Puerto Rico's revolt, but Cuban rebels continued to engage in **guerrilla** warfare for a decade. Spain tried to improve conditions by abolishing slavery and promising other reforms, but the promises were not kept.

Cuban soldiers in trenches awaiting the Spaniards, Pinar del Rio, Cuba

Joseph Pulitzer

YELLOW JOURNALISM

Joseph Pulitzer's newspapers included a comic strip called "The Yellow Kid." Later the Hearst newspapers ran another version of the strip. Sometimes the yellow ink used to color the Yellow Kid's clothing smeared across the pages. This color became linked with the sensational reporting and reckless editorials that both newspapers favored, a style that was nicknamed "yellow journalism."

To keep Cuban peasants from aiding the rebels, the Spanish military governor placed them in concentration camps. More than 100,000 people died in these camps from disease, starvation, and punishment. American newspapers reported Spain's brutality, urging U.S. **intervention**. Competing publications, especially **William Randolph Hearst**'s *New York Journal* and **Joseph Pulitzer**'s *New York World*, **sensationalized** the stories to sell more newspapers. These papers were known as the "yellow press."

William Randolph Hearst

American businessmen wanted Spain out of the Caribbean and pressed Congress to declare war. President McKinley did not want war, but a sudden event in February 1898 changed his mind. This was the sinking of the American battleship, the **USS** *Maine*.

Wreckage of the USS Maine

The *Maine* was in Havana with the permission of the Spanish government. On February 15, 1898, it mysteriously exploded and sank, killing 260 men. The newspapers claimed to have evidence that Spain had sunk the ship. Even though no evidence was found, most Americans were convinced that this was true. Later it was concluded that the explosion was probably caused by stored ammunition spontaneously igniting.

Spain tried hard to avoid war, but after the sinking of the *Maine* there was no option. In April, Congress authorized President McKinley to go to war. McKinley declared his intention to blockade Cuba's northern coast, and in response Spain declared war. On June 14, 17,000 U.S. soldiers landed on Cuban shores. Six weeks later, U.S. troops invaded Puerto Rico, easily defeating the Spanish.

Meanwhile, President McKinley had also sent troops to the Philippines. This was a country of about 7 million people spread over 7,083 islands (only 1,000 were inhabited) that reached across 660,000 square miles (1,709,400 sq km) of ocean. On May 1, Commodore **George Dewey** attacked and destroyed the Spanish fleet in Manila. On June 18, the Philippine commander declared independence. Meanwhile, three other U.S. ships captured Guam, which is 1,600 miles (2,575 km) east of Manila. The United States also claimed **Wake** Island in 1898 and later built a telegraph station there for communication between San Francisco and the Philippines. Guam and Wake are in a direct line between the Philippines and California and were seen as key defense points.

The Battle of Manila

On July 4, 1898, the United States defeated the Spanish fleet in Santiago, Cuba, ending the war. It had lasted barely four months. On July 16, Spain surrendered Cuba, and the next day the U.S. flag was raised in Santiago. In December, the United States and Spain signed the **Treaty of Paris**. The United States took over Puerto Rico, Guam, and the Philippines, paying Spain $20 million for the Philippines. Although the treaty officially granted Cuba independence, the United States installed a military government there that lasted until May 1902.

U.S. forces had suffered 5,462 casualties, but only 379 of them were from battle wounds. Most of the other deaths were from diseases such as malaria. American businessmen, including stock speculators, real estate agents, adventurers, and promoters, rushed to Cuba intending to get rich. The United Fruit Company took over the sugar industry. By 1901, Bethlehem Steel and other American companies had control of 80 percent of Cuba's minerals.

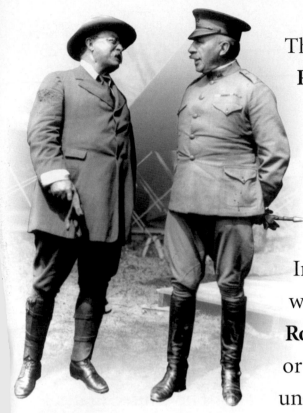

Theodore Roosevelt, left, and General Leonard Wood

The United States passed the **Platt Amendment** in 1901, which became part of the new Cuban constitution. It gave the United States the right to intervene in Cuban affairs and to establish naval bases. In 1901 General **Leonard Wood** wrote to President **Theodore Roosevelt**, "There is, of course, little or no independence left Cuba under the Platt Amendment." Under this amendment, the United States established the Guantánamo Bay naval base on Cuba's southeast coast.

After the war, the United States, once a colony itself, now found itself a colonial power. This came about partly because of the **Monroe Doctrine** of 1823, which stated that the United States would not tolerate European colonialism in the Americas. In 1904 President Roosevelt stated that the United States had the right and duty to exercise "international police power" in Latin America to correct "flagrant cases of wrongdoing." This became known as the "big stick" policy.

ACCESS TO FOREIGN MARKETS

Several years after the Spanish-American War, an American Department of Commerce official wrote, "Underlying the popular sentiment... [about defending liberty in Cuba] were our economic relations with the West Indies and the South American republics... It was seen to be necessary for us not only to find foreign purchasers for our goods, but to provide the means of making access to foreign markets easy, economical and safe."

By 1898 the United States was selling 10 percent of its produce, worth $1 billion, overseas. Farm products, especially tobacco, cotton and wheat, had long depended on international markets. Oil became a big export during the last two decades of the nineteenth century. By 1891 the Standard Oil Company controlled 70 percent of the world's **kerosene** market. As foreign markets became viewed as important to prosperity, **imperialism** had greater appeal to the American people.

Oil wells along the California coast

29

Congress now had to figure out how to define and manage its territories. It set up two types of territory, "incorporated" and "unincorporated." In the first type, inhabitants had the same rights as U.S. citizens. In the second type, Congress swore to respect the fundamental rights of native peoples, but not to hold them equal to U.S. citizens.

William McKinley

WHAT TO DO WITH THE PHILIPPINES?

Controlling Manila allowed a foothold in the Far East and access to the huge Chinese market. President McKinley justified the policy by saying, "We could not give [the islands] back to Spain—that would be cowardly and dishonorable. We could not turn them over to France or Germany, our commercial rivals in the Orient—that would be bad business and discreditable. We could not leave them to themselves—they were unfit for self-government... There was nothing left for us to do but to take them all and to educate the Filipinos, and uplift and civilize and Christianize them..." Later he told a group of ministers visiting the White House, "The truth is I didn't want the Philippines, and when they came to us as a gift from the gods, I did not know what to do with them..."

Puerto Rico was declared an "unorganized territory." Puerto Ricans were not considered U.S. citizens but were entitled to American protection. The U.S Congress and a federally appointed governor could veto bills passed by the Puerto Rican legislature. In 1917 Puerto Ricans became U.S. citizens who could choose their own legislators.

When Filipinos learned that the Treaty of Paris gave the United States possession of their island, they revolted. The United States took four years to suppress the uprising, with 20,000 Filipino combat deaths and 250,000 more dead of hunger and disease. More than 5,000 Americans also died. In 1902 the Philippines became an unincorporated territory. In 1916 Congress granted the Philippines independence once it formed a stable government. But except for three years of Japanese occupation during World War II, the American flag flew over Manila until 1946, when the Republic of the Philippines came into being.

Some Americans opposed imperialism, believing it was not in keeping with democracy. They said nations or cultures should not be taken over just because they are weak. An Anti-Imperialist League with 500,000 members was formed in 1898. It published letters and reports about the cruel behavior of U.S. soldiers in the Philippines.

After Hawaii was annexed, President McKinley said that a canal through the **Isthmus of Panama** would be essential to trade. In 1901, Theodore Roosevelt became president upon the assassination of McKinley. Two years later, Roosevelt helped revolutionaries in the Isthmus break Panama, a Colombian province, off from Colombia. He then negotiated a treaty with the Republic of Panama that let the United States build and maintain a canal linking the Atlantic and Pacific oceans in a "canal zone" 10 miles (16 km) wide. The provisions of the treaty essentially made Panama a colony of the United States in exchange for $10 million and an annual payment to Panama. The canal opened in 1914, but only in 1999 did Panama take full possession of the Canal Zone.

A steam shovel at work digging the Panama Canal

Another territory in the Caribbean Sea, the **U.S. Virgin Islands**, was purchased from Denmark in 1917 for $25 million. It includes three of nine main islands—St. Croix, St. Thomas, and St. John—and about 50 tiny islets. The other six islands in the chain, along with 25 islets, belong to Great Britain. About 109,000 people live in the U.S. Virgin Islands, which are a popular vacation spot for Americans. About 70 percent of the islanders work in tourism-related industries. Since 1927 they have been U.S. citizens. They elect their own governor and a one-house legislature and have a nonvoting representative in Congress.

Virgin Islands National Park

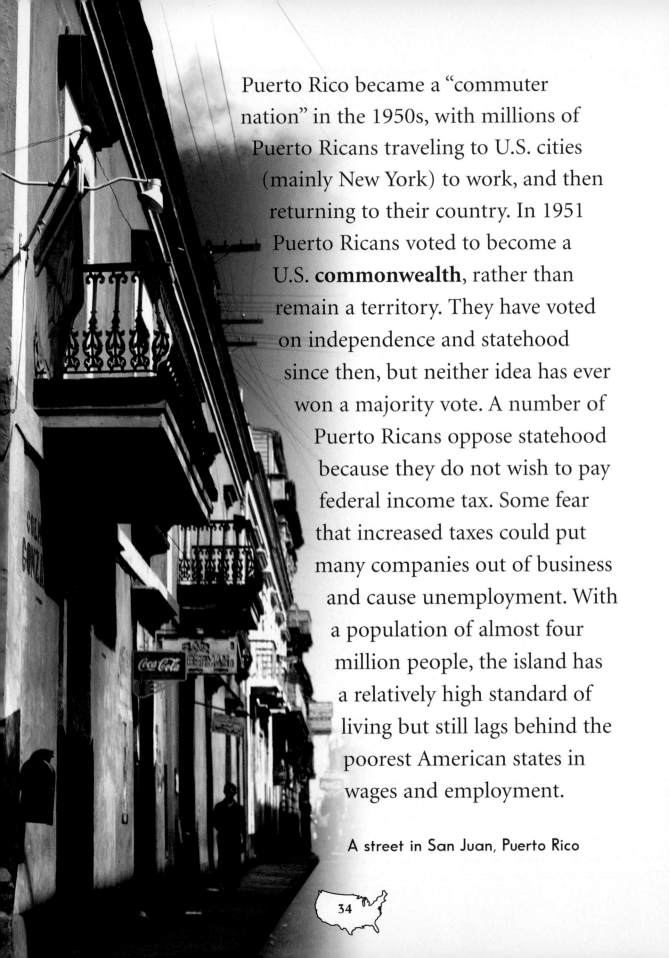

Puerto Rico became a "commuter nation" in the 1950s, with millions of Puerto Ricans traveling to U.S. cities (mainly New York) to work, and then returning to their country. In 1951 Puerto Ricans voted to become a U.S. **commonwealth**, rather than remain a territory. They have voted on independence and statehood since then, but neither idea has ever won a majority vote. A number of Puerto Ricans oppose statehood because they do not wish to pay federal income tax. Some fear that increased taxes could put many companies out of business and cause unemployment. With a population of almost four million people, the island has a relatively high standard of living but still lags behind the poorest American states in wages and employment.

A street in San Juan, Puerto Rico

Chapter IV: THE PACIFIC ISLANDS

A native in the Marshall Islands

After the Spanish-American War, Spain was left with the Caroline and Marshall Islands in the Pacific Ocean. Spain sold them to Germany in 1899, but Germany lost them to Japan in World War I. After World War II, the United Nations placed them under U.S. protection as part of the **U.S. Trust Territory of the Pacific Islands**.

This "trust territory" consisted of about 2,100 islands scattered across a vast expanse of water. Also called Micronesia, it stretched over an area as wide as the continental United States. It included three major **archipelagoes**, the Marshall Islands, Caroline Islands, and Mariana Islands. To administer these islands, they were divided into six districts: the Marshalls, Ponape, Truk, the Marianas, Yap, and Palau, and later Kusaie.

Testing nuclear weapons at Bikini Island

The Marshall Island chain contains 70 square miles (181 sq km) of **atolls** and reefs that cover about 4,500 square miles (11,655 sq km) of ocean. In the 1940s and 1950s, the United States tested more than 60 nuclear weapons there, causing dozens of people to die from radiation poisoning. The islands of **Bikini** and **Eniwetok** were evacuated. Hundreds were removed from Kwajalein Atoll to make way for **intercontinental ballistic missile** tests. In the 1970s islanders were allowed to return. They were evacuated from Bikini again in 1978 because blood testing showed dangerous levels of radiation.

The Mariana Islands were first named "Islas de los Ladrones" ("islands of thieves") by **Ferdinand Magellan** in 1521 because of an unfortunate encounter with the natives who lived there. Guam, the largest island in the Marianas, is an unincorporated, organized U.S territory. It is not considered part of the Northern Marianas. Until 1949, the U.S. Navy administered Guam except during World War II, when the Japanese occupied the island from 1941 until 1944. Today, U.S. naval and air force bases take up one-third of the land, and more than 23,000 of Guam's 106,000 people are U.S. military personnel.

The Trust Territory was dissolved in 1990. In the years before or after this date, islands and island groups formed a variety of relationships with the United States. Each district voted on what kind of status it preferred. Today these islands make up four separate, self-governing districts, as follows.

(1) The Northern Marianas form a U.S. commonwealth. Residents are U.S. citizens.

(2) Kusaie (now Kosrae), Ponape (now Pohnpei), Truk (now Chuuk), and Yap joined together in the Federated States of Micronesia.

(3) The Marshall Islands and

(4) Palau (Belau) decided to become republics.

Map showing the Federated States of Micronesia

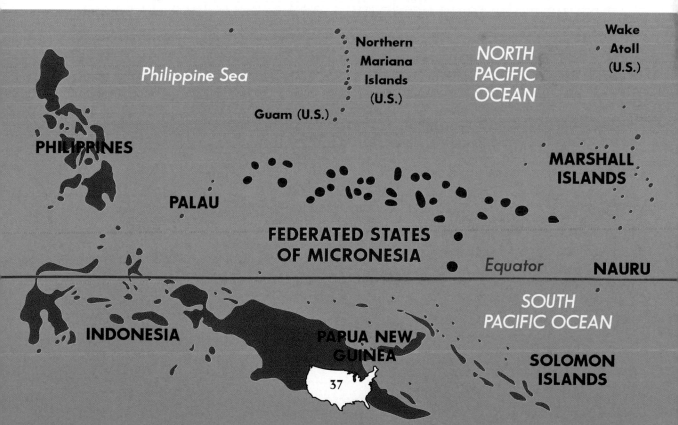

A harbor in the Mariana Islands

Except for the Marianas, these districts have "compacts of free association" with the United States. They allow self-government, but there are special trade benefits, and the United States is in charge of their defense. The United States pays their governments millions of dollars for the right to maintain military bases there.

Palau, Ponape, Truk, and Yap are the largest islands in the Caroline chain, which has more than 900 islands altogether. Fishing is the main occupation, and exports include **cacao**, **tapioca**, and dried **bonito**. Palau is now a self-governing group of 200 islands, only eight of which are inhabited.

U.S. military landing on Tinian, Mariana Islands

As part of its agreement with the United Nations, the United States promised to advance the region's people toward self-sufficiency. However, this policy has largely backfired. For example, the 60,000 Marshall Islanders have received $1 billion in recent years and are now totally dependent on U.S. payments. Thousands of people have left for Guam and Hawaii, seeking work.

American Samoa, about 2,600 miles (4,184 km) south of Hawaii, was acquired in 1900. It is an unincorporated, unorganized U.S. territory that served as a U.S. Marines staging area in World War II. It is largely self-governing and its inhabitants are U.S. **nationals**, not U.S. citizens. The territory's main trading partner is the United States, and canned tuna is its main export.

The United States also controls and administers groups of tiny islands—Howland, Baker, and Jarvis Islands; Kingman Reef; and Johnston, Palmyra, Wake, and Midway Atolls, all in the Pacific.

A Japanese tuna boat on a reef near Pago Pago in American Samoa

THE PACIFIC IS "OUR OCEAN"

Lack of understanding of other cultures led to racial prejudice in the United States. One Senator said "The Pacific is our ocean... China is our natural customer... The Philippines give us a base at the door of all the East... It has been charged that our conduct of the war has been cruel. Senators, it has been the reverse... [We] must remember that we are not dealing with Americans or Europeans. We are dealing with Orientals."

Baker, Howard, and Jarvis Islands were valuable in the nineteenth century for **guano**, which was used as a fertilizer. The air force used **Johnston Atoll**, about 700 miles (1,125 km) southwest of Hawaii, to conduct missile test launchings, and it is contaminated with plutonium. Also, the military has destroyed more than four million pounds of chemical weapons on Johnston Atoll since 1990.

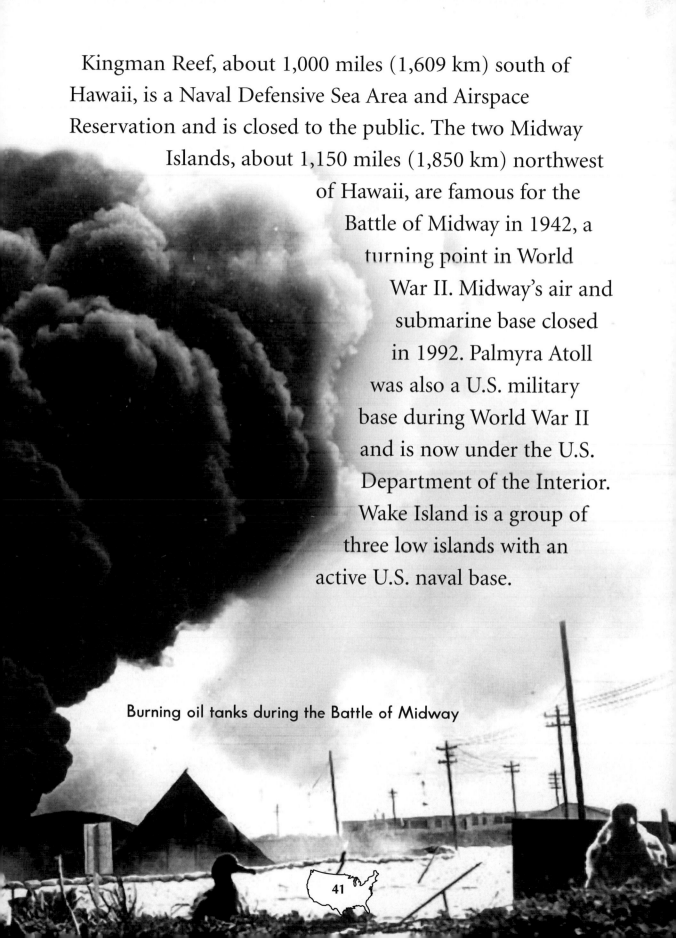

Kingman Reef, about 1,000 miles (1,609 km) south of Hawaii, is a Naval Defensive Sea Area and Airspace Reservation and is closed to the public. The two Midway Islands, about 1,150 miles (1,850 km) northwest of Hawaii, are famous for the Battle of Midway in 1942, a turning point in World War II. Midway's air and submarine base closed in 1992. Palmyra Atoll was also a U.S. military base during World War II and is now under the U.S. Department of the Interior. Wake Island is a group of three low islands with an active U.S. naval base.

Burning oil tanks during the Battle of Midway

U.S. territories have helped the United States defend itself, especially in the Pacific. Today, however, all of the territories are less well off than any state. Their citizens have varying degrees of rights and privileges, but they do not enjoy equal democratic status with U.S. citizens. The only U.S. territory that seems likely to become a state someday is Puerto Rico. On the other hand, Puerto Ricans could eventually vote to remain a commonwealth or become an independent country.

A municipal housing project in Puerto Rico

Over the years, Congress has tried to compensate territories for their unequal status by giving their residents citizenship, nonvoting delegates to Congress, a certain amount of local self-government, favorable tax treatment, trade benefits, and other advantages. Except in Puerto Rico, however, efforts to raise the economic status of territories have been disappointing.

Each U.S. territory has a unique history and culture, as well as a strong desire to control the effects of development on that special culture. This is usually difficult when decisions are made in Washington, D.C. For example, much of Guam's agricultural land was taken for U.S. bases after World War II. As a result, the people became dependent on imported food, largely from the United States. More than a quarter of **Guamanians** work for the government. If the United States should leave the island, its economy would suffer greatly. Balancing all of these factors to attain economic stability, cultural preservation, and self-determination is the present challenge for Guam and other U.S. territories.

A Timeline of the History of
UNITED STATES *Territories*

1787   Congress passes the Northwest Ordinance, setting rules for forming territories and states.

1820   American businessmen begin a sugar industry in the Hawaiian Islands, an independent monarchy.

1823   President James Monroe formulates the Monroe Doctrine, declaring that European colonialism will not be tolerated in the Americas.

1848   President James K. Polk offers $100 million for Cuba, but Spain rejects the offer.

1862   Congress encourages westward expansion, passing the Homestead Act.

1868   The United States buys Alaska from Russia; rebellions begin against Spanish colonialism in Puerto Rico and Cuba.

1890s   Gold discoveries in Alaska draw more settlers.

1893   American companies support a revolution that overthrows Hawaii's monarchy.

1898   The sinking of the USS *Maine* causes the Spanish-American War. The United States seizes Puerto Rico. U.S. fleets defeat Spain in Cuba and the Philippines. The United States takes Guam and also claims Wake Island. The Treaty of Paris of 1898-99 makes the United States a colonial power. Congress extends the Homestead Act to Alaska. Hawaii becomes a U.S. territory.

1899   Spain sells the Caroline and Marshall Islands to Germany.

1899-1900   The United States acquires American Samoa through a treaty with Germany and Great Britain.

1901   James D. Dole founds Hawaii's pineapple industry. In Cuba, American companies dominate the economy.

1902   With the Platt Amendment in force, the U.S. government withdraws from Cuba. The Philippine rebellion is suppressed, and the Philippine Islands become a U.S. territory.

1903   Border dispute between Alaska and Canada is resolved in favor of the United States. President Theodore Roosevelt aids rebels in freeing Panama from Colombia, with the aim of building a canal on the isthmus.

1904	President Theodore Roosevelt declares that the United States has the right to exercise "international police power" in Latin America, turning the Monroe Doctrine into a "big stick" policy.
1906	Alaska is named a territory.
1914	The Panama Canal opens.
1914-1918	World War I, in which canned Alaska salmon is an important export. Japan conquers the Marshall and Caroline Islands.
1916	Congress begins the process of giving the Philippines independence.
1917	Puerto Ricans become U.S. citizens. The United States purchases the eastern Virgin Islands from Denmark.
1927	U.S. Virgin Islanders become U.S. citizens.
1935	First hearings on Hawaii statehood are held in the House of Representatives.
1940	Extensive military build-up in Alaska and Hawaii.
1941	A Japanese air attack on Pearl Harbor brings the United States into World War II; martial law is in effect in Hawaii until 1944.
1947	The United Nations combines several groups of islands into a trusteeship, the Trust Territory of the Pacific Islands, to be managed by the United States.
1945-1950s	The United States tests more than 60 nuclear weapons in the Marshall Islands.
1946	The Philippines become an independent country.
1951	Puerto Rico becomes a U.S. commonwealth.
1955-56	Alaska creates and ratifies a state constitution.
1959	Alaska and Hawaii become the 49th and 50th states.
1979	Truk, Yap, Ponape, and Kusaie form the Federated States of Micronesia (FSM).
1982	The FSM, Palau, and the Marshall Islands sign compacts of free association with the United States.
1990	The United Nations ends the trusteeship of the Pacific Islands. Palau and the Marshall Islands become republics. The Northern Marianas become a U.S. commonwealth.

GLOSSARY

advocate - To plead in favor of; one that pleads the cause of another.

Aleut - Native people of the Aleutian Islands and western Alaska.

Aleutian Islands - Island chain off southwestern Alaska.

American Samoa - Eastern group of the Samoan Islands in the central Pacific.

annex - To add to something earlier, larger, or more important; to attach.

appropriate - To set apart or assign to a particular purpose or use.

archipelago - An expanse of water with many scattered islands.

Arctic Circle - The line of latitude that is approximately 66.5 degrees north of the equator.

atoll - A coral island that consists of a reef surrounding a lagoon.

Bikini - An island in the Marshall Islands, which was used for atomic bomb testing.

bonito - A type of fish that is in between a tuna and a mackerel.

cacao - The dried seeds of a South American tree that are used to make chocolate and cocoa.

Civil War - War between factions inside a country; the American Civil War (1861-1865) over the right to own slaves.

Cold War - The ideological conflict between the United States and the Soviet Union from the mid-1940s through the 1980s.

commonwealth - An association of self-governing states, often linked with a larger political entity that provides certain services such as defense.

Communist Party - An organized political party that advocates eliminating private property, owning goods in common, and making them available as needed.

compact - An agreement or covenant between two or more parties.

Confederate - An alliance; the group of southern states that seceded from the United States and fought the Union Army over slavery in the Civil War.

Eniwetok - Atoll in the northwest Marshall Islands.

Eskimo - A member of a group of native people of northern Canada.

Filipino - A native or citizen of the Philippine Islands.

folly - Lack of good sense; foolishness.

Guam - An island in the southern Mariana chain in the west Pacific Ocean.

Guamanian - Referring to a native of Guam.

guano - Seabird excrement, used as a fertilizer.

guerrilla - From the Spanish word for war, *guerra*, a person who fights in an often undeclared war, carrying out harassment and sabotage.

Homestead Act - U.S. legislation of 1862, which granted 160 acres (65 hectares) to anyone who would live on it and improve it for five years or more.

imperialism - The policy and practice of extending the supremacy of a nation by acquiring land or taking over the political or economic life of other areas; building an empire.

inflation - An increase in the volume of money with respect to goods and services causing a continuous rise in prices.

intercontinental ballistic missile (ICBM) - A missile that is guided in flight and free-falling in descent and capable of traveling between continents.

internment - The confinement of people, especially during war.

intervention - The interference with, or coming between, often by force of threat.

Inuit - The Eskimo people of North America and Greenland.

Isthmus of Panama - The narrow strip of land that connects Central America with South America.

Johnston Atoll - Atoll in the Central Pacific Ocean, southwest of Hawaii.

judiciary - A system of courts of law.

kerosene - A flammable oil, usually obtained from petroleum, which is used for fuel.

legislator - A member of a lawmaking body.

martial law - The law applied by a governing body in occupied territory.

Micronesia - Islands of the west Pacific including the Caroline, Marshall, and Mariana groups, among others.

monopoly - Exclusive ownership or control.

Monroe Doctrine - U.S. foreign policy written by John Quincy Adams in 1823, presented to Congress by President James Monroe. It asserted that the Americas were no longer open to European colonization.

national - A person who is under the protection of a nation without being a citizen.

nationalism - Extreme loyalty and devotion to a nation to the point of promoting that nation's interests above all others.

Northwest Ordinance - U.S. law of 1787 that described when settled land could become a territory or a state and defined the rights of people living there.

Oahu - An island in the Hawaiian chain, site of the capital city, Honolulu.

Pacific Fleet - An organization of U.S. ships and aircraft stationed in the Pacific Ocean.

Palau - Island group in the Caroline Islands, known locally as Belau.

Pearl Harbor - Inlet of Oahu just west of Honolulu; site of a U.S. Navy base.

Platt Amendment - Legislation in 1901 that was designed to regulate U.S.-Cuba relations, permitting U.S. intervention and providing a U.S. naval base in Cuba.

prejudice - Injury resulting from a decision or action that affects one's rights.

Puerto Rico - "Rich port" in Spanish, the name of a self-governing U.S. commonwealth in the West Indies, former U.S. territory.

ratify - To formally approve or confirm.

sensationalize - To present in a manner that is emotional, exciting the senses, rather than rational, appealing to the mind.

Spanish American War - Conflict between the United States and Spain waged in 1898 in the West Indies and Philippines.

tapioca - A granular form of a tropical plant starch, often used in puddings.

territory - A geographical area; an area under U.S. control with a separate legislature but not yet a state.

Tlingit - A Native American people of the islands and coast of southern Alaska.

Treaty of Paris - Several historical treaties have this name; in this case, the treaty ending the Spanish American War in 1898.

U.S. Trust Territory of the Pacific Islands - Large area in the Pacific Ocean comprising more than 2,000 islands, mostly in Micronesia, which was placed under U.S. control by the United Nations in 1947.

U.S. Virgin Islands - The western islands of the Virgin Islands group in the West Indies, which make up a U.S. territory.

USS *Maine* - U.S. battleship mysteriously blown up and sunk in Havana Harbor in February 1898 in an incident that triggered the Spanish American War.

Wake - An island in the northern Pacific, north of the Marshall Islands, that belongs to the United States.

KEY PEOPLE IN THE HISTORY OF *U.S. Territories*

Dewey, George - (1837-1917) U.S. Spanish American war hero, promoted to admiral in 1899.

Dole, James D. - (1877-1958) Founder of the Hawaiian Pineapple Co.

Eisenhower, Dwight - (1890-1969) 34th president of the United States.

Ginaca, Henry - (1876-1918) Designer of the Ginaca machine to process canned pineapple.

Hearst, William Randolph - (1863-1951) U.S. publisher who owned 18 newspapers along with magazines and radio stations.

Johnson, Andrew - (1808-1875) 17th president of the United States.

London, Jack - (1876-1916) U.S. novelist and short-story writer, born John Griffith.

Magellan, Ferdinand - (1480?-1521) Portuguese explorer in the service of Spain, discovered the Philippines in 1521 and was killed there by natives.

McKinley, William - (1843-1901) 25th president of the United States.

Polk, James K. - (1795-1849) 11th president of the United States.

Pulitzer, Joseph - (1847-1911) U.S. journalist and founder of the Pulitzer prizes.

Roosevelt, Franklin - (1882-1945) 32nd president of the United States.

Roosevelt, Theodore - (1858-1919) 26th president of the United States.

Seward, William H. - (1801-1872) U.S. statesman who served as Abraham Lincoln's and Andrew Johnson's secretary of state.

Takahashi, Sakae - (1919-2001) Member of 100th Infantry Battalion, winner of Bronze Star and Purple Heart.

Wood, Leonard - (1860-1927) Major general who commanded the 1st Volunteer Cavalry in the Spanish American War; served as military governor of Cuba until 1902.

INDEX

Books of Interest

Aylesworth, Thomas G. and Virginia L. Aylesworth. *Territories and Possessions (Discovering America)*, Chelsea House Publishers, 1995.

Kent, Deborah. *Hawaii's Road to Statehood (Cornerstones of Freedom)*, Children's Press, 2004.

Kristen, Katherine. *Pacific Islands (Portrait of America)*, Steck-Vaughn Company, 1996.

London, Jack. *The Call of the Wild*, Aladdin, 2003 (originally published in 1903).

McNair, Sylvia. *U. S. Territories (America the Beautiful)*, Children's Press, 2001.

McNeese, Tim. *Remember the Maine: The Spanish-American War Begins (First Battles)*, Morgan Reynolds Publishing, 2001.

Santella, Andrew. *Pearl Harbor (We the People)*, Compass Point Books, 2004.

Somervill, Barbara A. *Alaska (From Sea to Shining Sea)*, Children's Press/Scholastic, 2002.

Web Sites

http://www.pbs.org/crucible/

http://www.smplanet.com/imperialism/toc.html

http://college.hmco.com/history/readerscomp/rcah/html/ah_041000_hawaiiannexa.htm

http://www.theus50.com/alaska/

Linda Thompson is a Montana native and a graduate of the University of Washington. She was a teacher, writer, and editor in the San Francisco Bay Area for 30 years and now lives in Taos, New Mexico. She can be contacted through her web site,

http://www.highmesaproductions.com

48